Be a Fantastic Realtor

Sell more real estate by understanding your clients' wants and needs

Gail Cassidy

Copyright © 2013 by Gail Cassidy. All rights reserved.

This book or any portion thereof may not be reproduced or used in any manner whatsoever without the express written permission of the publisher except for the use of brief quotations in a book review.

Disclaimer and Terms of Use:

The Author and Publisher has strived to be as accurate and complete as possible in the creation of this book, notwithstanding the fact that he does not warrant or represent at any time that the contents within are accurate due to the rapidly changing nature of the Internet. While all attempts have been made to verify information provided in this publication, the Author and Publisher assume no responsibility for errors, omissions, or contrary interpretation of the subject matter herein. Any perceived slights of specific persons, peoples, or organizations are unintentional.

Printed in the United States of America, First Printing,

Tomlyn Publications
547 Shackamaxon Drive
Westfield, NJ 07090
http://www.coachability.com

Be a Fantastic Realtor

Sell more real estate by understanding your clients' wants and needs

Table of Contents

TIPS FOR REAL ESTATE AGENTS 5

PHILOSOPHY 7

ATTITUDE 9

HUMAN RELATIONS 11

COMMUNICATION 13

SELF ESTEEM 15

DISCIPLINE 17

SELLING TREASURE TIPS 19

TIPS FOR BROKERS 21

TIPS FOR ALL STAFF 23

WORTHY QUOTES 25

HE KEPT RIGHT ON TALKING 27

TEN WAYS TO ENHANCE SELLING IN YOUR AGENCY 29

INFORMATION INTERVIEW 31

TEN FAMOUS FOOTBALL QUOTES FOR REAL ESTATE 33

TIPS FOR REAL ESTATE AGENTS

Being a real estate agent can be a wonderful, satisfying, and potentially lucrative profession, but it is also one that can be filled with challenges and frustrations. Within these pages are ideas and tips that could help anyone become even more successful.

Realtors need a tremendous amount of knowledge, specialized knowledge in Lead Marketing, Telephone Prospecting, Listing Marketing, Referral Marketing, Database Marketing, Closing Strategies, and Personal Management, i.e., being organized, plus much more.

In spite of realtors' extensive training, several national tests have revealed the following startling statistics about why salespeople fail:
15%: Improper training, both specialized and sales skills.
20%: Poor verbal and written communication skills.
50%: Attitude!

Attitude is how we see things; how we feel about things. Attitude is like the steering mechanism in our brains. And the nice thing is, we all have the ability to control our attitudes.

Think of the bumble bee. According to recognized aeronautical facts, because of the size and weight of its big body in proportion to its little wings, the bumble bee shouldn't be able to fly. But the bee doesn't know that.

The point is we can learn from the bee. We can do anything if we change our attitudes about life. In life, it is not what happens to us; it is how we react to what happens to us that counts.

I have found the following tips to be relevant for almost all daily situations involving human interactions. Dealing with potential buyers and sellers requires a thorough knowledge of human relation skills as well as legal and professional real estate skills, but hopefully the majority of realtor/buyer interactions are of a positive, constructive, and rewarding nature.

Enjoy reading the tips. Highlight those you want to keep in the forefront of your mind. Enjoy your clients. Their unique plights, their individual perspectives, and their unusual predicaments will provide you with the gift of never-ending memories.

Warmly,
Gail

PHILOSOPHY

1. See the invisible tattoo on every person's forehead that reads: **"PLEASE MAKE ME FEEL IMPORTANT."**

2. Find at least one happening in each client experience to be grateful for.

3. Look for positives in every person you meet.

4. Recognize the specialness of diversity.

5. Provide an atmosphere conducive to selling, e.g. a smile, politeness, etc.

6. Vary your daily responses. Do something different that people will remember.

7. Remember, humans of any age cannot listen and absorb for extended periods of time.

8. Get buyers and sellers excited about buying and selling. Everyone has a hot button.

9. Understanding each client is when you learn.

10. Learn the Serenity Prayer: "God, grant me the serenity to accept the things I cannot change, courage to change the things I can and the wisdom to know the difference."

11. "See" and/or "feel" your positive day before you begin via positive self-talk.

12. Be (or act) enthusiastic about everything you do. It's contagious; it carries over to your clients.

13. Accept people as they are, and then provide the atmosphere for them to follow the law.

14. Learn from every colleague, every good and challenging client.

15. Ask yourself, "Does it really matter?"

16. Being right does not always work, e.g.,

> Here lies the body of William Jay, who died maintaining his right of way. He was right, dead right as he sped along, but he's just as dead as if he were wrong.

17. **HAVE FUN!**

ATTITUDE

18. Park your ego at the door; it hinders relationships with people you encounter.

19. Give your clients a reason to check their negative attitudes also.

20. Know that people "mirror" you. They reflect what they see, hear, and feel from you.

21. Shake things up. Make changes. "If you always do what you have always done, you'll always get what you've always got."

22. Show people through your own example what fun having a great attitude is.

23. Be patient.

24. Positive attitudes are catching.

25. Show respect to get respect.

26. Know that attitude is a choice everyone makes every day.

27. Explain that people cannot help what happens to them, but they are always in charge of their responses.

28. Remember, there is a pause between stimulus and response. Choose your response carefully.

29. Ask negative clients why they are choosing to be the way they are.

30. Know that attitude is the steering mechanism of the brain. Body language can lead to attitude.

31. Practice changing your attitude by sitting or standing straight, with your head up, and a smile on your faces. It does work!

32. Know that it is the attitude of our hearts and minds that shape who we are, how we live, and how we treat others.

33. Help people to recognize their specialness.

34. Success is feeling good about yourself every single day. That is attitude.

35. Know that true power is knowing that you can control your attitude at all times.

HUMAN RELATIONS

36. Treat potential trouble makers as if he or she were your friend's friend.

37. Never talk down to anyone.

38. Find what is special about every person.

39. **SMILE.** It warms a heart.

40. Use tact when responding to a challenging client. The rewards outweigh "being right."

41. Know that it is not in your best interests for anyone to feel your negativity.

42. Be 100% fair at all times--no exceptions.

43. Keep in mind that perception is reality--yours and your clients.

44. Treat every person you meet as you wish to be treated.

45. Understand that no one wants to be wrong.

46. Everyone desperately wants to feel special.

47. Remember that people gravitate toward things that are pleasurable and avoid things that are painful. Make obeying rules pleasurable.

48. **LISTENING** is the greatest compliment.

49. Try to understand before being understood.

50. Show genuine appreciation to all of your clients and co-workers.

51. Begin corrective action with sincere and honest recognition of what has been done correctly.

52. Never embarrass someone unnecessarily. Allow the person to save face.

53. Use encouragement. Make the error seem easy to correct.

54. Don't be afraid to admit your mistakes. It will make you appear more human to people.

55. Show respect for every person's opinion.

56. Challenge people to be the best that they can be.

57. **Make SINCERITY your No. 1 priority**.

COMMUNICATION

58. Set standards in your area of responsibility and share them with the people you work with.

59. Personalize the reasons a client should buy and a seller should sell.

60. Set high expectations. Remember the story of the new teacher who thought the locker list from 140-160 was the list of IQ's in her class and she treated them accordingly, and they performed accordingly. Treat clients and co-workers in the same way.

61. Know that 55% of all messages comes from the body. Notice how you can tell your special someone is in a bad mood without any words being spoken.

62. Know that 38% of the message comes from the voice: inflection, intonation, pitch, speed, e.g., "I didn't say he stole my prospect." Seven words = seven meanings.

63. Know, you cannot **NOT** communicate.

64. Recognize that we don't all see the same thing when looking at the same thing.

65. Know also that we don't all hear the same things even when listening to the same words.

66. Control your thoughts; your feelings come from your thoughts; therefore, you can also control your feelings! Choice is control.

67. Teach yourself to take responsibility for what you say and how you say it.

68. Listen for the message, yet know that body language can be interpreted as only a clue to the meaning of the message, e.g., arms crossed in front of chest could mean blocking you or could mean person is actually cold or comfortable.

69. Learn to lead rather than to try and overcome resistance.

70. Communicate your enthusiasm through your body and voice.

71. "One who is too insistent on his own views, find few to agree with him." -Lao-Tze

72. Speak with a warm heart.

SELF ESTEEM

73. Know that a person with high self-esteem does not need to find fault with others.

74. Know that people find fault with others when they feel threatened, consciously or unconsciously.

75. Know that self-esteem is not noisy conceit. It is a quiet sense of self-respect, a feeling of self-worth. Conceit is whitewash to cover low self-esteem.

76. Remember, **people have two basic needs: to know they are lovable and worthwhile.**

77. Remember, it is the person's feeling about being respected or not respected that affects how s/he will behave and perform.

78. Helping people build their self-concept is helpful in successful selling.

79. Know that your words have power to affect a person's self-esteem.

80. Each person values himself to the degree s/he has been valued.

81. Words are less important in their affect on self-esteem than the judgments that accompany them.

82. The attitude of others toward a person's capacities are more important than his possession of particular traits.

83. Bragging people are asking for positive reflections.

84. Masks are worn to hide the "worthless me."

85. Low self-esteem is tied to impossible demands on the self.

86. A realtor's own self-acceptance frees him or her to focus on the client, unencumbered by inner needs.

87. The single most important ingredient in a nurturing relationship is honesty.

88. Ask this: "If I were to treat my friends as I treat my clients and co-workers, how many friends would I have left?"

89. Avoid mixed messages. Be clear in your statements of expectations.

DISCIPLINE

90. Tolerate no disrespect.

91. Be consistent in enforcing rules.

92. Set boundaries.

93. Find opportunities for each negative client to improve his/her behavior.

94. Differentiate between the action and the person.

95. Uncover and address, when possible, the reasons for the person's negativity.

96. Make sure clients have the ability to understand.

97. Focus, as often as possible, on what is right rather than what is wrong.

98. Give plenty of recognition for the unique gifts of each client and co-worker.

99. Teach your clients and co-workers to know they have power in the present moment to change their thoughts, feelings, and attitude at any time.

100. Remind clients and co-workers to take control of their lives by focusing on the present.

101. Remove the word "try" from people's vocabulary. Have them "try" to pick up a pencil. Either they do or they don't.

102. Work with clients to find the lesson or value in unacceptable situations.

103. Make sure clients know they have choices in spite of their past experiences.

104. Set an example by turning any problem into a learning opportunity.

105. Make sure clients are clear about the positives and negatives of the situation.

106. Approach problematic clients with relaxed confidence.

107. Being a model for your clients and co-workers to follow provides them with a picture of what appropriate behavior looks like.

108. Respond thoughtfully to challenging and/or problem situations--avoid making judgments.

109. Teach problem solving:
- State the problem
- Look for causes of the problem
- Brainstorm solutions
- Choose the best one

110. Encourage people to see beyond their own point of view.

111. Encourage habits of thought conducive to growth in understanding others, to think outside the box.

112. Recognize that there is no one interpretation of an incident.

SELLING TREASURE TIPS

113. Know that you too are special.

114. Enjoy each day and each client.

115. When possible, make corrections by citing two positives for every negative.

116. Make your sales presentations relevant to your clients' needs and wants.

117. Be alert to teachable moments.

118. Show lively enthusiasm!

119. Create an atmosphere of fun.

120. Build on successes.

121. Create a routine with varied activities.

122. Turn clients on to improving their community.

123. Encourage yourself to visualize doing well.

124. Have a relaxed demeanor.

125. Make everyone feel important.

126. Give one instruction at a time.

127. Give people opportunities to succeed.

128. Provide a safe atmosphere.

129. Validate people frequently.

130. Recognize the positive value of competition in selling.

131. Recognize that people are on a quest for identity and some sense of personal power.

132. Above all, enjoy each day. You are the mirror.

TIPS FOR BROKERS

• Validate your staff on a regular basis, not just during a once-a-year review.

• Tell staff members specifically what you like about what they are doing. They will work harder to earn that recognition again in the future.

• Encourage workers to strive for excellence. "We are what we repeatedly do. Excellence, then, is not an act but a habit." - Aristotle.

• Encourage agents to align their goals with their values. Conflict arises when the two are in conflict.

• Expect the best from your staff. People live up to expectations.

• Always abide by the golden rule: "Do unto others as you would have them do unto you."

• Involve as many agents as you can in community activities. Those who participant feel more a part of the "family."

• Always always be fair.

• Avoid being judgmental.

• Treat your staff to bagels one morning a week. Let them know you care.

- Encourage agents to use their powers of observation and logic. Successful agents see details and discover principles that others do not.

- Encourage and enable agents to continually grow. Complacency breeds stagnation.

- Make your community an inviting place to work.

- Make your staff proud to be a part of your "family."

TIPS FOR ALL STAFF

- Work towards feeling good about yourself. It is man's highest goal.

- Always do what you feel is right or true.

- . Your actions reveal your values.

- Your thought is the most powerful force in your universe. "Nothing is either good or bad but thinking makes it so."
- Shakespeare.

- Whatever you dwell on expands.

- Work toward goals that cause you to feel a sense of mastery.

- Write a list of everything you have accomplished or have been recognized for in your life. Add to it whenever you think of something new. Read it when the going gets tough.

- Have a clear sense of purpose in life.

- Clarify your goals and focus on them

- Be a risk taker. Step outside your comfort zone. Try something new.

- Polish your people skills.

- Hone your communications skills.

- Take excellent care of yourself.

- Positive expectations are the single, most outwardly identifiable, characteristics all successful people possess.

- Your reality is what you make it to be.

- You can train yourself to think more positively by training yourself to choose what you pay attention to and what you say about it, both to yourself and others. "We know what we are but know not what we may be." -Shakespeare.

- Whatever you believe, picture in your mind, and think about most of the time, you eventually will bring into reality.

- Your self-image is the most dominant factor that affects everything you attempt to do.

- Nothing is more exciting than the realization that you can accomplish anything you really want that is consistent with your unique mix of natural talents and abilities.

WORTHY QUOTES

- Assume a virtue, if you have it not. - Shakespeare.

- Act enthusiastic and you'll be enthusiastic. -Carnegie.

- Begin to be now what you will be hereafter. - St. Jerome. Repetition is the mother of skill.

- It is not the place, nor the condition, but the mind alone that can make any one happy or miserable. - L Estrange.

- Beliefs have the power to create and the power to destroy. - Robbins.

- Nothing is more likely to help a person overcome or endure troubles than the consciousness of having a task in life. -Frankl.

- When the student is ready, the teacher will appear. - Zen proverb.

- The ancestor to every action is a thought. -Emerson.

- Imagination is more important than knowledge. -Albert Einstein.

- Sell so that you won't be ashamed to sell your parrot to the town gossip. - Will Rogers, adapted.

- Selling does not make an agent, it reveals him(her). - James Allen, adapted.

- Things do not change; we change. -Thoreau.

- Change your thoughts and you change your world. -Norman Vincent Peale.

- Great men are those who see that thoughts rule the world. -Emerson.

- Nothing has any power over me other than that which I give it through my conscious thoughts. -Anthony Robbins.

- The greatest discovery of my generation is that human beings can alter their lives by altering their attitudes of mind. -Wm James.

- You are what you choose today. -Dyer.

- The agent who is attempting to sell without inspiring the client with a desire to follow them is hammering on cold iron.

- The only limits you have are the limits you believe. -Wayne Dyer.

- Anything we fail to reinforce will eventually dissipate. -Robbins

- Patience is the companion of wisdom. -Augustine.

- The more he gives to others, the more he possesses of his own. -Lao-Tze.

- Vision is the art of seeing things invisible. -Swift.

- What the mind can conceive and believe, it can achieve. -Hill.

HE KEPT RIGHT ON TALKING

With all the relevant specialized training out of the way, we have to remember the importance of listening and being aware of our client's reactions. We, too, may lose a sale if we keep right on talking. This humorous poem illustrates the point.

"His arguments were well received.
His point had, clearly, been achieved.
And his sincerity had quelled
All reservations that I held.
I would have signed the order, then,
If he had just produced a pen.
But he kept right on talking.

 Couldn't he see he'd raised my hopes
That I was hanging on the ropes?
He had me sold and, man alive,
The time to close had now arrived.
I wanted desperately to sign,
If he would just point out the line.
But he kept right on talking.

And then my mind began to stray
To pressing matters of the day.
His voice, now growing even higher
In his enthusiastic fire,
Became distraction, then a bore.
I couldn't take it any more.
But he kept right on talking.

I stood, to bring it to an end.

"My time is limited, my friend."
"But, Sir, I thought--, he numbly said.
"You thought that I was interested?
Perhaps I was, but not today."
I didn't have the heart to say,
He's killed his sale by talking.

It is a paradox, but true.
Though talk can bring success to you.
Oh, what a tragic thing to see,
The source of failure it can be.
So if you want the winner's cup
You'll make your point, then shut up,
And not keep right on talking.

Written by Harry O. Hamm, Beverly Hill, CA

TEN WAYS TO ENHANCE SELLING IN YOUR AGENCY

GOALS: Create community through the sharing of ideas; develop leadership; promote excellence, and prepare agents to the best of their abilities.

1. Give each real estate agent a copy of *Be a Fantastic Real Estate Agent*.

2. Personalize the booklets with your logo.

3. Have copies available for community members.

4. Include a booklet in each new staff member's packet.

5. Use for discussion at meetings.

6. Encourage agents to use these concepts for research.

7. Ask agents to add to the lists.

8. Use individual lists as topics for general discussion. Find out where there is agreement and where there is not.

9. Use these principles as the basis for your agency's standards.

10. Study the various lists and add new points and new topics. This will be an opportunity to expand the consciousness of agents and their brokers.

INFORMATION INTERVIEW

DETERMINE AREAS OF TRAINING NEEDED BY HAVING REALTORS COMPLETE THE FOLLOWING:

- What stands in the way of your employees making more money, selling more houses?

- What personal or organizational behaviors would you like to see changed in your employees?

- How are their phone manners?

- What are their attitudes like?

- How professionally do they act?

- How professionally do they dress?

- How are their time management skills?

- How are their communication skills?

- How are their listening skills?

- How are their writing skills?

- How is their attendance in the office?

- How well do they focus?

- What areas would you like to have the focus on?

- How is their interaction with one another?

- How could their wok lives be easier?

- How could their work lives be more productive?

- Do employees know what they want?

- Do employees have a vision?

- What is your vision?

If you could have anything in the next 90 days, what would that be?

TEN FAMOUS FOOTBALL QUOTES FOR REAL ESTATE

1. "Do right. Do your best. Treat others as you want to be treated."--Lou Holtz

2. "Without self-discipline, success is impossible, period."--Lou Holtz

3. "I learned that if you want to make it bad enough, no matter how bad it is, you can make it." --Gale Sayers

4. "Build up your weaknesses until they become your strong points."--Knute Rockne

5. "Show class, have pride, and display character. If you do, winning takes care of itself."--Paul "Bear" Bryant

6. "The difference between a successful person and others is not a lack of strength, not a lack of knowledge, but rather in a lack of will." --Vince Lombardi

7. "The road to Easy Street goes through the sewer."--John Madden

8. "If a team is to reach its potential, each player must be willing to subordinate his personal goals to the good of the team."--Bud Wilkinson

9. "Football is an honest game. It's true to life. It's a game about sharing. Football is a team game. So is life."--Joe Namath

10. "Winning isn't everything, but it beats anything that comes in second."--Paul "Bear" Bryant

"The agent's character is one of his/her most effective agents of persuasion."
adapted, Aristotle

May you all have a stellar sales year!!!

For information on how to personalize copies of this Tips book for your agency, please contact gail@coachability.com.

www.ingramcontent.com/pod-product-compliance
Lightning Source LLC
Chambersburg PA
CBHW071553170526
45166CB00004B/1654